Producer
Rick Quattrini

Photography by Neil Sutherland
CLB 1699
© 1986 Illustrations and text: Colour Library Books Ltd.,
   Guildford, Surrey, England.
Text filmsetting by Acesetters Ltd., Richmond, Surrey, England.
Printed and bound in Barcelona, Spain by Cronion, S.A.
All rights reserved.
ISBN 0 86283 467 8

NEW YORK
ON THE WATER

Text by
Bill Harris

CLB

When Frédéric Auguste Bartholdi came to the United States in 1871 to gather support for his colossal sculpture *Liberty Enlightening the World*, he traveled up and down the Eastern Seaboard and as far west as the Great Salt Lake, but never for a moment did he think of any other site for his statue than Bedloe's Island in the Upper Bay of New York harbor, the most prominent spot in the gateway to the New World.

He would site his statue so that anyone rounding the Narrows between Brooklyn and Staten Island would see her off in the distance, seemingly striding forward in eager welcome. As a ship wended its way through the nearly seven-mile-long channel to the Manhattan anchorages, she would always be there on the port side burning into the memory. And as a ship passed directly in front of her an arriving immigrant would suddenly notice that this figure that had been striding forward, torch in hand, was now standing erect, saluting the promise of America. The movement is in the mind's eye, of course. And in one's soul.

Even Americans who have never seen the Statue of Liberty know her as one of the most enduring symbols of their country. And people all over the world regard her as a goal to be attained. The setting has a lot to do with the drama she inspires, and though today's immigrants are more likely to fly over her than sail past her, the emotional experience of the 19th-century immigrants is recreated every day of the week as thousands make pilgrimages into the harbor aboard vessels ranging from the Staten Island Ferry to luxurious yachts, where they sip fine French wines and contemplate this wonderful gift of the people of France to the people of the United States.

New York harbor itself might be called a gift of the king of France, though it was more an act of indifference than generosity. The first European to sail through the Narrows and up the Hudson River was the Florentine Giovanni da Verrazano, who arrived in 1524 in an expedition financed by Francis I of France. The Italian explorer had named the river "Grand," but the king seems to have been unimpressed. Though he sent several other expeditions to confirm Verrazano's enthusiasm, he never claimed the harbor or the river for France. In fact, a Portuguese sailing for Spain had already renamed the river "Rio de Gomez" in honor of himself.

The name stuck until 1609, when an Englishman named Henry Hudson arrived aboard a Dutch ship and wrote in his log that the surrounding territory was "as beautiful a land as one can hope to tread upon." The Delaware Indians who were already there had known that for several hundred years and had long since discovered the advantages of the wonderful, well-protected harbor at the end of what they called "The River That Flows Both Ways."

The Dutch brought civilization to the place and gave the river yet another name, "North River," to distinguish it from the Delaware, which marked the southern boundary of their territory in the New World.

Though the Dutch built a wall across the north end of their settlement to keep the English from marching on them from New England, the harbor itself provided an open door for a British fleet that sailed through the Narrows in 1664 and took the place without a fight. They renamed the settlement "New York," and honored their countryman by naming the great river "Hudson."

The Hudson River was the birthplace of the steamboat at a time when it was already the prime destination of the great American clipper ships. The harbor provided a safe haven for some 20 million souls in search of a better life. The great ocean liners that symbolized the good life for travelers in the early 20th century were made greater by their association with the Port of New York.

But, to many of us in the 1980s, the harbor and the river are at their best as a thing of beauty, a backdrop for New York's incredible skyline, a place to get a relaxed view of the vitality of the greatest city on the face of the earth, a city that got its greatness from its position at the gateway to a New World.

The adventure begins over dinner with the sun going down behind the Statue of Liberty casting a pink glow over the Brooklyn piers. Then, (overleaf) the necklace of lights on the Brooklyn Bridge adds a touch of pure romance.

Previous pages: **Riveranda** *and* **Empress of New York** *are as much a part of New York Harbor as the Statue of Liberty herself. The views of bridges and piers from* **Riveranda's** *Promenade Deck (above) are, as the song says, "just made for a girl and boy." So is twilight in the Upper Bay (overleaf), where the Lady in The Harbor has welcomed ships of every description for a hundred years.*

PARADE OF SAIL JULY 4, 1986

U.S.C.G. Bark
EAGLE
U.S.A. 295'

DANMARK
(Denmark)
252'7"

CHRISTIAN RADICH
(Norway)
241'

LIBERTAD
(Argentina)
365'8"

ZENOBE GRAMME
(Belgium) 95'

BLUENOSE II
(Canada)
160'6"

ESMERALDA
(Chile)
370'8"

GLORIA
(Colombia)
249'3"

GUAYAS
(Ecuador)
257'6"

BELEM
(France)
190'9"

DEWARUCI
(Indonesia)
191'3"

GALAXY
(Israel)
120'

AMERIGO VESPUCCI
(Italy)
331.416

CUAUHTEMOC
(Mexico)
296'10"

SORLANDET
(Norway)
216'

SHABAB OMAN
(Oman)
170'

SAGRES II
(Portugal)
293'

JUAN SEBASTIAN DE ELCANO
(Spain)
370'

SVANEN OF STOCKHOLM
(Sweden)
92'

CALIDA
(Scotland)
135'

CAPITAN MIRANDA
(Uruguay)
197'

SIMON BOLIVAR
(Venezuela)
270'

ELISSA
(USA)
202'

GAZELA OF PHILADELPHIA
(USA)
177'

Spirit of
Massachusetts
125'

Westward
125'

American Rover
125'

American Eagle
114'

Bowdoin
88'

Belle Blonde
165'

Pilot
155'

Angelique
125'

Clipper City
158'

La Dame De Canton
85'

Bel Espoir II
122'

Regina Maris
144'

Rambler
110'

Corsaro II
66'

New Way
130'

Anna Kristina
108'

Rachel & Ebenezer
105'

Sherman Zwicker
142'

Harbinger
126'

Pioneer
102'

Puritan
197'

Victory Chimes
102'

Rose
170'

Mystic Clipper
130'

Pride of
Baltimore
136'

Elinor
118'

Alexandria
125'

Ernestina
152'

Clearwater
106'

National
Convention
102'

Roseway
135'

Te Vega
156'

Shamrock V
127'

Rara Avis
124'

Belle Lurette
65'

Ring Anderson
114'

Nathaniel
Bowditch
100'

Felice Manin
66'

Harvey Gamage
115'

Anne Kristine
93'

Lady Ellen
177'

Barba Negra
110'

Providence
110'

Fri
107'

Blackjack
90'

Bounty
169'

Mystic Whaler
123'

Previous pages: the Queensboro Bridge crossing Roosevelt Island and the Communipaw Ferry Terminal (inset) overlooking Manhattan from Jersey City's Liberty State Park are among the sights reflected in New York's waters (this page), as are South Street Seaport (facing page), and (overleaf) Battery Park, the Staten Island Ferry and the towers of Lower Manhattan.

*The view from **Riveranda's** bridge includes (facing page, top) Turtle Bay in the East River at 42nd Street where the U.N. Secretariat Building shares the midtown skyline with landmarks like the spire-topped Chrysler Building. The view also includes the USS **Intrepid** (facing page, bottom) in the Hudson River at 42nd Street. Now a museum, the aircraft carrier is one of the most decorated ships in U.S. naval history. Overleaf: luncheon is served aboard **Riveranda** in the shadow of the Brooklyn Bridge, where the nearby sights include South Street Seaport, with its new Pier 17 and its permanent fleet of tall ships, and the bubble-topped piers of the Wall Street Racquet Club.*

*Previous pages: even at night the Port
Authority piers at the edge of Brooklyn
Heights are usually a beehive of activity.
But their lights don't hold a candle to the
buildings in Manhattan's Financial District.
Facing page:* **Riveranda** *almost never sails
anywhere without passing close to the
Statue of Liberty, even when she voyages
out to the edge of Long Island Sound and
under the Bronx-Whitestone Bridge
(below). She often cruises past Riverside
Church (overleaf) overlooking the Hudson
River from Manhattan at 121st Street, or
Shanghai Red's Restaurant on the Hudson
in Weehawken, New Jersey. And, of course,
no voyage is complete without going
beneath the Brooklyn Bridge.*

Previous pages: the Statue of Liberty, the harbor itself, is beautiful at any time of the year. But in winter when the air is crisp and the water flecked with ice, her beauty is something special. This page: though the Great Hall and dining room in Ellis Island's main building became quiet and forbidding with the ravages of time, to most of the thousands who passed through the immigration facility it was a place of rare beauty and the welcome was very warm, indeed. Overleaf: the Binghampton Restaurant in Edgewater, New Jersey, was once an Erie Railroad ferry operating between Hoboken and Manhattan. She was powered by hand-stoked coal burners. Today's vessels are clean enough to sport white tablecloths.

Previous pages: one of the very best things about New York is the sunsets. No two are ever quite alike, none is ever anything but strikingly beautiful. But no New York sunset is ever better than one seen from the water, especially when the buildings reflecting the glow are the World Trade Center towers, the World Financial Center and the rest of the Financial District. This page: whether the view is of the George Washington Bridge over the Hudson River or the edge of Murray Hill in the mid-30s on the East River, the best way to enjoy it (facing page) is while enjoying a fine lunch. The lunch adventure could take you past the United Nations complex (overleaf) on the East River at 42nd Street.

*This page: cruising up the East River is a lot more fun than driving up the FDR Drive, and if you begin at the beginning, you'll see South Street Seaport the way it was intended to be seen. Facing page: Pier A, the fireboat station at the edge of Battery Park, is not only Manhattan's oldest pier, it is one of the oldest continuously-operating fire stations in the United States. The beautiful building at the other side of the park is the old U.S. Customs House. The house at the edge of the East River in the lower picture is Gracie Mansion. It's where the mayor lives. Overleaf: a taste of the good life is represented by **The Highlander**, a yacht owned by Malcolm Forbes of **Forbes** Magazine. The inscription on the side of the helicopter identifies it as a "capitalist's tool." The inscription at the base of the Statue of Liberty hardly seems necessary.*

THE
STATUE
OF LIBERTY

Erected in 1886, the Statue, "Liberty Enlightening the World", was a gift from the people of France. United States citizens raised funds for the stone pedestal on which it stands. Conceived as a monument to the long friendship between France and the United States that began during the American Revolution, the Statue has become a beacon of hope for newcomers to America.

Previous pages: the ghost of an old ferry terminal pier lives under the Brooklyn Bridge as a reminder of what was once the only way to get to Brooklyn from Manhattan. When the bridge was built, its stone towers were the tallest structures in either Brooklyn or New York, which were separate cities back then. This page: they call this "The Street of Ships," but in the days when it was a working port, South Street Seaport wasn't this slick. Facing page: back in those days, they didn't have floating restaurants sailing past, either. And what the floating restaurant gives its diners besides memorable meals is close-up contact with one of the great symbols of New York, scrappy little tugboats like the one heading down the East River past Roosevelt Island. Overleaf: the latest addition to South Street Seaport, Pier 17, provides a wonderful place to sit and watch the tugs go by. Like the rest of the Seaport, it's a good place to eat and shop, too.

The Fulton Fish Market is an old New York institution that gets better all the time. It's only a short distance downriver from The U.N. (facing page) and Roosevelt Island. Overleaf: the insets show the red lighthouse under the George Washington Bridge and the city of Edgewater, New Jersey, just across the bridge.

Previous pages: looking at the Empire State Building from the top of Rockefeller Center or the downtown skyline and Statue of Liberty from an incoming jet, nothing beats the view from the water (facing page). And (this page) the vessels with the best views are **Riveranda** *and* **Empress of New York***. Though neither of them can show you Lower Manhattan from the air or (overleaf) Roosevelt Island from above, there is no view in the world like New York on the water.*